Jungle

Tim Vicary

Oxford University Press

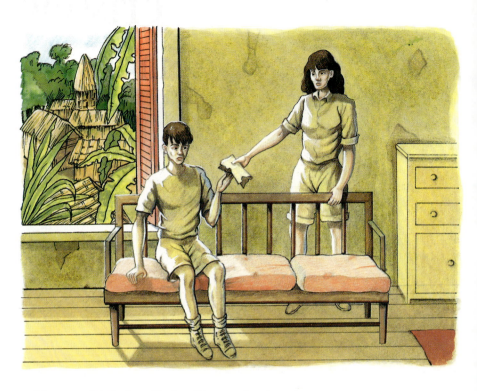

'Do you think that Dad will come back today, Karen?' John asked.

'I don't know, John,' Karen answered. 'Stop asking me. You ask me ten times a day and I've told you: I don't know when Dad's coming back!'

'But he's been away for two weeks now. It's a long time. Do you think something has happened, Karen? Do you think he's had an accident?'

Karen was quiet for a minute. 'Perhaps. I don't know. I just don't know.' Then she walked across the room and looked out of the window.

Karen was seventeen, and her brother John was fifteen. They were in Ruali, a small town in a country in Africa. Their father often went into the jungle to look for strange birds. But, usually, he went for two or three days – not for two weeks.

'John, I have a letter here. A man gave it to me this morning. It's from Dad.'

John looked at the letter. The paper was dirty, and there were holes in it; it was difficult to read. 'What does it mean?' he asked. 'I don't understand it.'

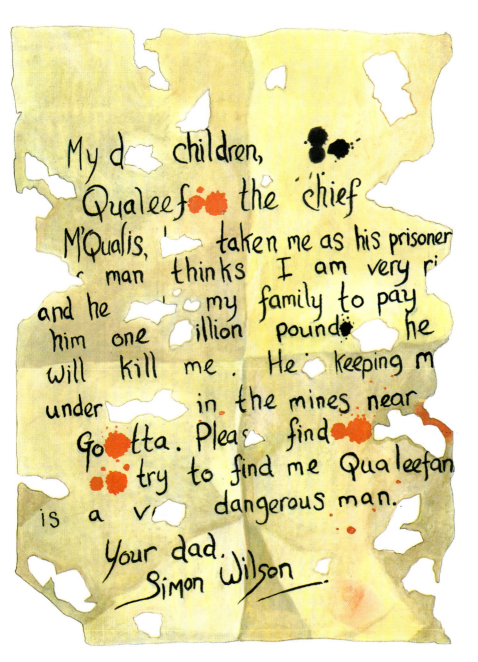

My d— children,
   Qualeef— the chief M'Qualis, — taken me as his prisoner
— man thinks I am very ri—
and he — my family to pay
him one — illion pound— he
will kill me. He — keeping m—
under — in the mines near
Go—tta. Pleas— find—
— try to find me Qualeefan—
is a v— dangerous man.
      Your dad.
      Simon Wilson

• Look at the letter. What does it say?

'I think that Dad has been kidnapped. Look! It says: "... has taken me as his prisoner" and "... thinks I am very rich" – and that must mean "a million pounds"! But that's impossible, John. Dad hasn't got much money!'

'Of course he hasn't. But he doesn't want us to pay. He wants us to find him. "Please try to find me" – that's what the letter says, isn't it?'

Karen shook her head. 'I don't know, John. It says that Qualeefan is a very dangerous man. Oh, poor Dad! But how can we find him? We don't know where he is!'

'Yes, we do!' John said. 'Look. This is the name of the town, isn't it? Oh no, there's a hole in the middle of the letter!'

'Never mind, let's look at the map,' Karen said. 'There aren't very many towns near us. I'm sure we can find it.'

She found a large map and opened it on the table. 'Now, this is where we are. Dad went on foot, so it can't be too far away. Help me look!'

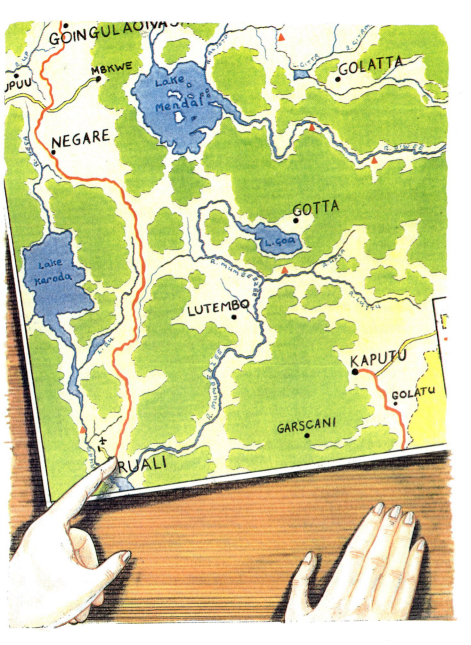

- Look at the map. Can you find the town where Simon Wilson is?

'OK,' John said. 'I agree. It's Golatta. But how does that help?'

'I think we should go there,' Karen said. 'When we've seen it, we can decide what to do.'

'But how can we get there?' John asked. 'It's a long way to walk, and this man Qualeefan is dangerous.'

'We'll go by plane, silly,' Karen answered. 'We'll ask Mr Bailey to fly us. He's Dad's friend. Then we can look at the town from the air. That'll be quite safe.'

Bill Bailey knew their father. He had a small plane at the airport outside Ruali. The children showed him the letter, and he agreed to fly them to Golatta.

They took off later that afternoon, and flew north-east. After ten minutes the sky turned black in front of them.

'That's a bad storm,' Bill Bailey said. 'I'm going to fly north to go round it.' He turned north and flew past the black clouds. Karen watched the storm go behind them.

After fifteen minutes Karen said, 'Can we turn east now?'

Bill Bailey shook his head. 'Not yet. We'll turn south-east in five minutes. That'll bring us to Golatta in twenty minutes.'

'I don't think so, Mr Bailey,' John said. He looked at the map carefully. 'There are a lot of islands in that lake, near the river mouth. I'm sure it's Lake Mendal. It's twenty kilometres west of Golatta, so we should turn east.'

Bill Bailey laughed. 'Nonsense! That's Lake Karoda. Those aren't islands, they're just clouds! I have flown planes here since you were a baby! Forget about the map. Just look out of the window and watch the trees!'

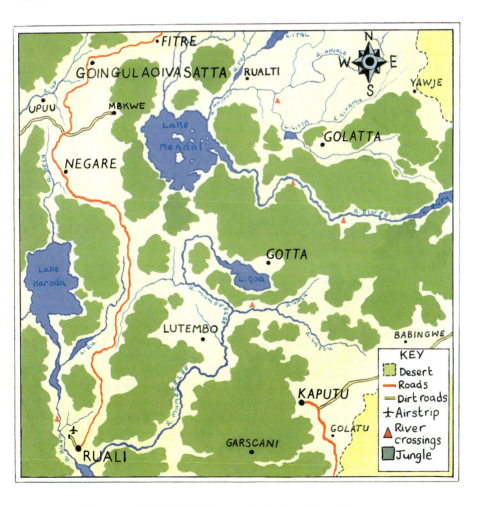

• Who was right? Which lake is below them?

They flew south-east. The storm was far away now, on their right. After fifteen minutes, they saw another lake below them, and a river running out of it. John looked at the map again.

'But that's the river Mumbeezee, Mr Bailey,' he said. 'I'm sure we're flying towards Gotta, not Golatta.'

'Nonsense,' Bill Bailey said. 'There's Golatta, right in front of us. Look!'

The plane flew low towards a small town. People came out into the streets and looked up. Some of them had guns in their hands.

'I hope it isn't Gotta,' Karen said. 'Dad told us that the people there are dangerous.'

'All these jungle towns look the same,' Bill Bailey said.

'Dad told us that there is a very tall building in Gotta,' John said. 'They put the bodies of dead people on top of it, and big black birds take them away. The building has a lot of trees round it.'

'Well, there's nothing like that here,' Bill Bailey said. He was beginning to get angry. 'For the last time, this is Golatta, I tell you! And there's the chief's house!'

Suddenly, there was a loud noise, and the plane moved to one side in the air.

• Look at the town below the plane. Is it Gotta, or Golatta?

'Bill! They're shooting at us!' Karen screamed. 'Quick – do something!'

'I am! I – aaaaaaaargh!' Bill screamed. The plane started falling on its side. Then Bill pulled back the joystick, and it went up again. The town disappeared behind them. But something was wrong with Bill. His face was white, and his eyes were closed.

'Bill,' Karen said. 'Bill? What's the matter, Bill?'

Bill didn't answer. He had one hand on the joystick, and the other hand on his stomach. There was a lot of blood on his shirt.

'Bill!' Karen said. 'John, help me – they've shot him!'

Bill fell forward in his seat. The plane began to fly straight down, towards the ground.

'Quick! Take him out of his seat!' Karen shouted.

John pulled Bill sideways, into another seat. Then Karen moved into Bill's seat, and pulled the joystick backwards, as hard as she could.

The plane began to climb back into the sky. Finally, it flew straight again.

'Well done, Karen!' John said. 'Now what? Can you turn the plane round and fly us home?'

'I don't know – I've never flown a plane before.'

'Well, remember what Mr Bailey did. Hold the joystick with your hands, and move the pedals with your feet to turn right or left.'

Karen tried turning the plane carefully. It worked. 'All right,' she said. 'Perhaps. But I don't know how to land.'

'We'll think about that later,' John said. 'But first, just keep the plane in the air. I'll check the instruments. I think everything is working. If we've got enough fuel, we'll be OK.'

• Look at the instruments. Is anything wrong?

'We haven't got any fuel!' John said. 'The engine will stop in a few minutes! What can we do? Can you land somewhere?'

'There's nowhere to land down there – nothing but trees and a river!' Karen was afraid. 'Ask Bill – Bill will have to do something!'

John looked at Bill Bailey. His face was very white and his eyes were closed. 'I – I think he's dead, Karen,' he said quietly.

'Well, we're going to die too,' Karen said. 'I can't land this plane in the jungle – it's impossible. No one could do that.'

'Wait.' John went to the back of the plane. 'Look here!'

'What have you got?'

'Parachutes. You put them on like this, jump out, and pull this cord.'

John put his parachute on quickly, and then sat in the pilot's seat while Karen put hers on. The plane's engine stopped.

Karen opened the door, and looked out. The forest was a long way below her, and the wind was very strong. She closed her eyes, and jumped.

She opened her arms wide, and counted slowly: one . . . two . . . three . . . four . . . five . . . She pulled the cord. Something pulled hard on her shoulders. She looked up, and there, above her, was a beautiful blue and white parachute!

And somewhere above her, there was another, smaller parachute, with John underneath it.

Suddenly, there was a loud noise above her head. She looked up and saw that her parachute was torn.

'Oh no!' she thought. 'The air is going straight through my parachute. What do I do now? I think there's a second parachute, but how do I open it?'

• Look at the instructions on Karen's parachute, and try to understand what she should do.

The trees came towards Karen very quickly. Suddenly she realized what she needed to do. She pulled the ring. With a loud noise the second parachute opened and she went down slowly towards the trees. Her feet went through the leaves, and a minute later she was on the ground.

'You're shaking,' said John, when he landed near Karen. 'Are you OK?'

'Yes, but that was horrible,' she answered.

'We'll be OK. Which way do we go? I don't know where we are.'

'I do. We go east towards the river. There are two places there where we can go across to the other side. Look, it shows them on the map. When we get there, we must look carefully to see if it's safe – sometimes there are crocodiles. Come on, follow me.'

They walked east for an hour, until they came to the river. The ground near the river was very wet, and the two teenagers could see a lot of animal tracks.

'Are there any people's tracks?' Karen asked, sounding afraid. 'If people have gone across here before us, I think it will be OK for us, too.'

'You look for them,' John said. 'I'm going to see if there are any crocodiles in the river.'

• Look carefully at the picture. Do you think it's safe to cross the river here?

There were no crocodiles, so they crossed the river with no difficulty.

'It's not far now,' John said. 'About five kilometres to Golatta.'

After an hour Karen saw a bag beside the path. She picked it up and opened it. There was a small book inside.

'What's this?' she said. 'It looks like . . .'

'Yes!' said John. 'It's Dad's diary. But a lot of the pages are torn or damaged.'

It was an old red book. They looked at it closely. It was about birds, but on the last page, something was written in code. Karen looked at it carefully for a minute, and then she got out a pencil and a piece of paper and began to write the message down. She smiled.

'That's it, John!' she said. 'Of course, I understand now!'

'What do you mean?' John asked. 'What does it say?'

'It's Daddy's own code – it's easy! Look at the front of the book!'

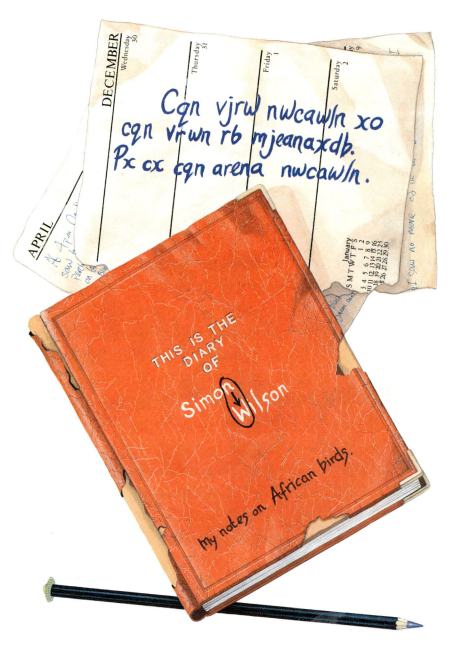

* How does the front of the book help Karen to read the code? What is the message?

'Fantastic!' John said. 'Now I understand what that word "mine" meant in Dad's letter!'

They walked through the jungle. They had to hide behind trees three times, because they heard the voices of people and didn't know if they were friendly or not. At the end of the day they were near a small river.

On the other side of the river there was a hill, and near the bottom of the hill there was a small door. As they watched, they saw an old man come out of the door in the hill. He closed the door behind him, locked it, and walked away.

'Look!' Karen said. 'That door goes into the mine.'

They waited until it was nearly dark, and then found a boat and crossed the river. There was a strange lock on the door, with a lot of numbers on it.

'How do we open this?' John asked. 'It's a very strong lock. We can't break it. And I can only move the numbers on the left.'

'Think, John,' Karen answered. 'You're good at maths. You can do it, can't you?'

'Probably,' John said. 'I can see that the column on the right adds up to fifteen. And I think the column in the middle is the same . . .'

'Be quick, John!' Karen said. 'I can hear someone coming!'

• Quick! Find the numbers to open the lock.

They opened the door. It was dark in the mine, but there was a small room on the left of the door. Karen and John went into the room, and found a lot of miners' hats, with lights on them. Karen and John each put a hat on, and switched on the light.

'Where do we go now?' John asked.

'Isn't this a map on the wall?'

'It doesn't look like an ordinary map,' John said. 'Some lines are red, some are green, and some are blue. What do they mean?'

Karen said, 'Perhaps the red lines are for the paths at the top of the mine, and the blue and green ones deeper under the ground.'

'Perhaps. Or perhaps the blue lines are the paths at the top. How do we know? Look – what are these pieces of paper on the table?'

'I don't know,' Karen said. 'I think some insects have torn them up.'

'There are still a lot of pieces here,' said John. 'Let's try to put them together.'

'Come on, John. We must be quick! We haven't got much time and we must find Dad. But where is he?'

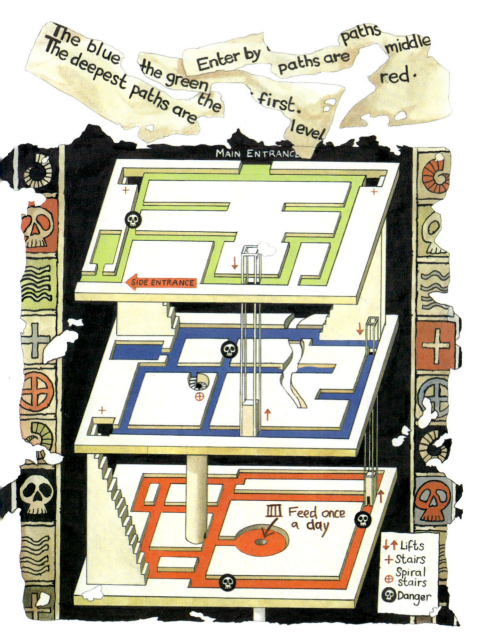

The blue
The deepest paths are
the green
the
Enter by
paths are
first.
paths
middle
red.
level

MAIN ENTRANCE

SIDE ENTRANCE

▥ Feed once
a day

↓↑ Lifts
+ Stairs
⊕ Spiral
stairs
☠ Danger

· What do the pieces of paper say? Where are Karen and John on the map? Where is their father and how do they get to him?

'I can see where we are now.' John was excited. 'We're in a green tunnel, and this is where we have to go. But how can we help Dad to escape?'

'Let's find him first,' Karen said. 'Come on!'

They took the map off the wall, and ran through the dark tunnels. They went down to the blue level in a lift. It was very quiet there. They could hear water going down the walls, and they could hear their feet on the ground. After a while the sound of water got louder and louder. Then they came round a corner, and the tunnel went under the water.

'What's this?' Karen said. 'This isn't on the map, is it?'

John looked at the map. 'No, I don't think so. But the map shows that the tunnel goes down a little here, and then up again . . .'

'Well, what are we going to do?'

'I don't know,' John said. 'I can swim underwater for twenty metres, I think.'

'So can I,' said Karen. 'But I don't think it's a good idea here – it looks dangerous, and it's very dark. Let me see the map again. There's some writing on it, isn't there?'

'Yes,' John said. 'But it's terrible handwriting. What does it say?'

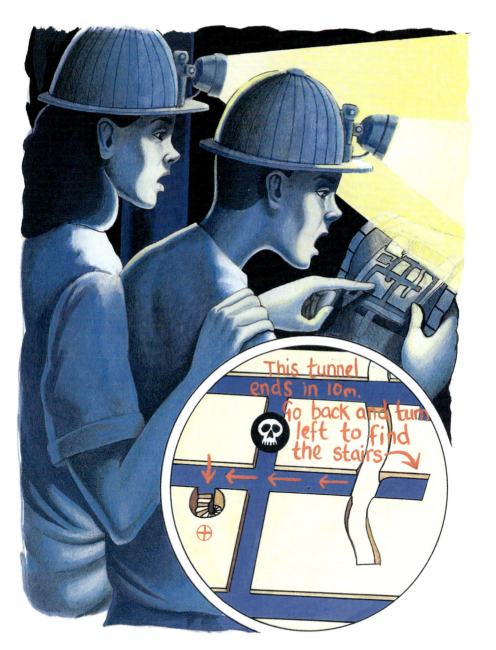

• Look at the map. What does it say? Do you think they should swim underwater, or find another tunnel?

'All right then, we'll look for the stairs,' John said. 'You're right, it's too dangerous to swim underwater in the dark, and the tunnel ends. We could die there.'

They turned back and soon they found the stairs. They went down and down and down, round the outside of a big hole.

'I'm afraid,' said John quietly.

'So am I,' answered Karen. 'But we have to find Dad.'

After a few minutes, they arrived at the bottom safely.

'It can't be far now,' Karen said. 'Oh, look!'

There was a big open room in front of them, and in the middle there was the biggest, most horrible dog they had ever seen. A long rope tied it to the wall. It had enormous teeth, and it looked very angry.

'Oh no,' said John. 'Perhaps it thinks we're food!'

'Well, we're not,' said Karen. 'And look – there's something strange about this dog. Why isn't it looking at us? What's wrong with its eyes?'

'Oh! I don't think it can see; it can only hear.'

'Yes, but it can still hurt you!' Karen said. 'Look at those teeth!'

'You stand here and talk to it, and I'll walk behind it very quietly.'

'I think I can see a place where it can't get me, even if it hears me,' John said. 'Don't worry.'

'I hope you're right,' Karen said. Then she began to talk to the dog. 'Good dog, good boy,' she said. 'Come here, you horrible animal. You can't hurt us. Oh, John, be careful!'

• Look at the picture, and find the path that John must use to escape the dog.

John moved to the side of the room. The dog made a terrible noise, and its enormous teeth looked like knives. It knew he was there, but it couldn't do anything to stop him. It was so angry that it made a table at the side of the room fall, and ate some papers that were on it. Karen followed the same path as her brother.

When she was on the other side of the room with John, they looked at the buttons for the lift.

'Dad is in the lift. How do we bring it up?' Karen asked.

'I don't know,' John said. 'There's probably water at the bottom of this hole. If we send the lift down, Dad will have a terrible accident. He might die!'

'There must be some instructions,' Karen said. 'What was that paper on the table?'

'The dog ate it,' John said. 'Look!'

He picked up four or five pieces of paper.

'But that's what it is,' Karen said. 'Instructions! We've got to read them! We mustn't make a mistake now!'

She put the pieces of paper on the table and looked at them. They were very difficult to read, because the dog ate some of the pieces . . .

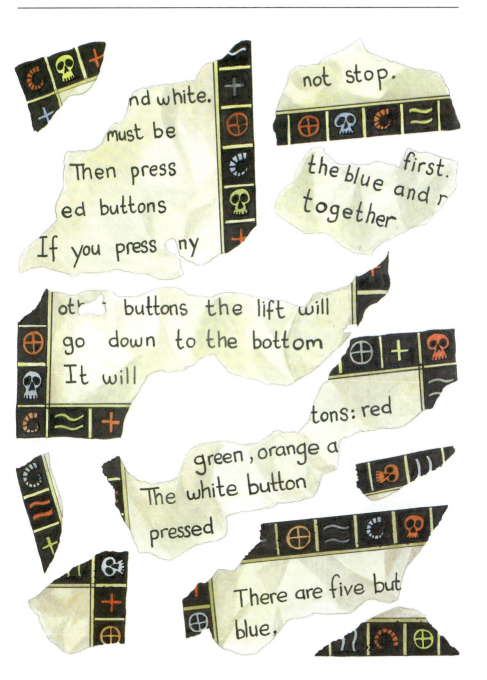

nd white.

must be

Then press

ed buttons

If you press ny

not stop.

the blue and r first. together

ot buttons the lift will
go down to the bottom
It will

tons: red

green, orange a

The white button

pressed

There are five but

blue,

- Can you read the instructions?

'Right, then,' John said. 'I think I understand it.'

'I hope you're right', Karen said. 'This could be a terrible mistake.'

John pushed the white button. At first nothing happened. Then a machine made a noise, but the ropes for the lift did not move.

'OK,' Karen said. 'Let's try this, then.' She pushed the red and blue buttons at the same time. 'Come on, lift,' she said. 'Come up, please!'

Karen and John looked down. Far away in the darkness, something was moving – up, towards them! A cage came out of the hole and stopped in front of them. There was a man inside it.

'Dad!' Karen said. 'Dad – it's us!'

The man looked out. His hand was in front of his eyes because the light was too bright for him. He opened the door of the cage.

'Karen?' he said. 'Karen – and John? Is it you?'

'Yes, Dad,' they said. 'We're here – we came to find you!'

He held them in his arms. 'Thank you,' he said. 'Oh, how wonderful! But how did you find me? No, first we must escape from here, and then you can tell me all about it.'

John looked at the cage, and the hole, and the terrible dog near the wall. He laughed. 'Well,' he said. 'That's going to be easy, isn't it. Much easier than getting in here!'

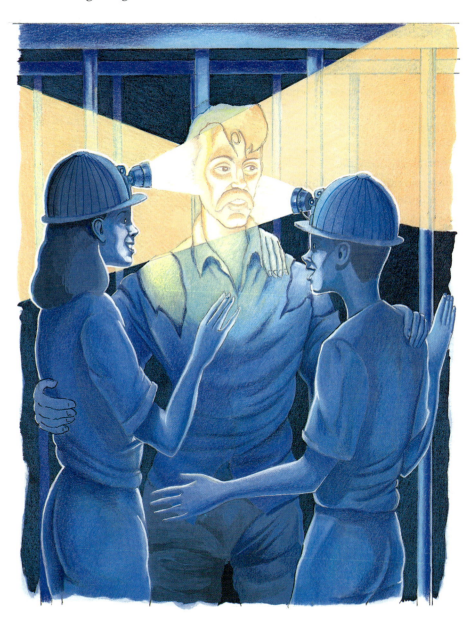

Glossary

button small, round thing on a machine

chief head of a group of people

code secret writing

column vertical line (of numbers)

damage break or hurt something

diary where you write what has happened each day

emergency a sudden, serious problem

enormous very big

fuel something you burn to make an engine work

joystick something in a plane that controls the direction it flies in

jungle thick forest, found in hot countries

kidnap take and hide someone so his family will pay money for him to return

level where something is, e.g. high or low

line row of something (numbers)

lock close something with a key

machine something with many parts that move together

main most important

message information that one person sends to another person

mine big hole in the ground that people make when they are looking for precious stones, etc.

miner person who works in a mine

nonsense silly ideas

parachute thing like a big umbrella that you wear when you jump out of a plane

path narrow way for people to walk on

pedal a control that you move with your feet

prisoner someone who is in a locked place

track rough marks that people, animals, etc. make when they walk along

tunnel long hole under the ground for a road or train

Answers to the puzzles

page 3
My dear children,
Qualeefan, the chief of the M'Qualis, has taken me as his prisoner.
This man thinks I am very rich, and he wants my family to pay him one million pounds, or he will kill me. He is keeping me underground in the mines near Golatta. Please find some money. Do not try to find me. Qualeefan is a dangerous man.
Your father, Simon Wilson

page 5
He is in golatta.

page 7
Lake Mendal

page 9
Gotta

page 11
There isn't any fuel.

page 13
In emergency only: pull this ring.

page 15
Yes, because there are tracks from people, but not from crocodiles.

page 17
The 'n' from 'Simon' becomes 'w'. So, 'o' becomes 'x', 'p' becomes 'y', etc. The message is:
The main entrance of the mine is dangerous. Go to the river entrance.

page 19

6	8	1
0	5	10
9	2	4

page 23
This tunnel ends after ten metres. Go back and turn left to find the stairs.

page 27
There are five buttons: red, blue, green, orange, and white. The white button must be pressed first. Then press the blue and red buttons together. If you press any other buttons, the lift will go down to the bottom. It will not stop.

page 21
The paper says: Enter by the green paths first. The blue paths are the middle level. The deepest paths are red.

page 25

Oxford University Press, Great Clarendon Street, Oxford OX2 6DP

Oxford   New York
Athens   Auckland   Bangkok   Bogotá   Buenos Aires
Calcutta   Cape Town   Chennai   Dar es Salaam   Delhi
Florence   Hong Kong   Istanbul   Karachi   Kuala Lumpur
Madrid   Melbourne   Mexico City   Mumbai   Nairobi   Paris
São Paulo   Singapore   Taipei   Tokyo   Toronto   Warsaw

and associated companies in
Berlin   Ibadan

OXFORD and OXFORD ENGLISH are trade marks
of Oxford University Press

ISBN 0 19 422480 5

© Oxford University Press 1992

First published 1992
Eighth impression 1999

Cover illustration by Paul Dickinson

Illustrated by Paul Dickinson

Typeset by Wyvern Typesetting Ltd, Bristol, England

Printed in Hong Kong